LYNTON & LYNMOUTH

A shortish guide

Colin Croxford

Bossiney Books · Launceston

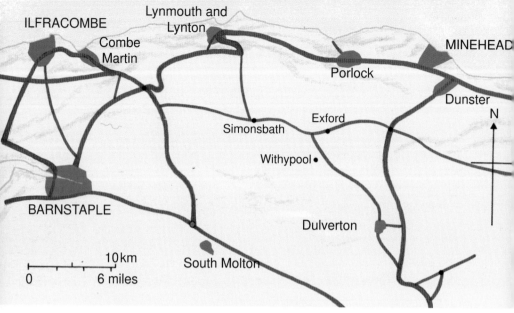

The setting of the twin villages of Lynton and Lynmouth on the North Devon coast makes them an ideal centre from which to explore the whole of the Exmoor National Park

Other Bossiney books about Exmoor

Exmoor, a Shortish Guide
Shortish Walks on Exmoor
Shortish Walks in North Devon
Pub Walks on Exmoor

First published 2008 by Bossiney Books Ltd
Langore, Launceston, Cornwall PL15 8LD
www.bossineybooks.com
ISBN 978-1906474-01-0
© 2008 Colin Croxford   All rights reserved

Acknowledgements
The maps are by Graham Hallowell
The cover is based on a design by Heards Design Partnership
The photographs are reproduced by kind permission as follows: pages 9 and 11
Lyndale Photographic Ltd; pages 16 and 31 Robert Hesketh.
All other photographs are from the publishers' own collection

Printed in Great Britain by R Booth Ltd, Penryn, Cornwall

Introduction

The twin villages of Lynton and Lynmouth are set in some of the most dramatic scenery found in the British Isles. Rivers fed from numerous streams on the high moor combine in their hurrying descent to meet with the sea at Lynmouth. Their erosive effect for millions of years has resulted in the deep valleys, now tree-lined and locally known as combes, which form a wonderful backdrop to the villages.

Looking out across the Bristol Channel, on a fine day the coastline of Wales is clearly visible, Porthcawl being almost due north at a distance of approximately 27 km (17 miles).

Historically Lynmouth, like a number of small harbour villages along the Bristol Channel coast, relied on this strip of water. Coal and other trade goods were imported, whilst lime, timber and fish were exported. For reasons which will be explained below, this suddenly changed. From around 1800, Lynmouth suddenly became a holiday destination for wealthy and discriminating people.

Lynton, 200 m (600 ft) above Lynmouth, grew as the popularity of Lynmouth flourished and suitable building sites for hotels by the harbour and in the valley were exhausted. It was transformed from a small farming community centred on the church to a tourist village with new hotels, boarding houses and domestic housing spreading west towards the Valley of Rocks. What you see today is largely the result of that Victorian and Edwardian expansion.

Geology

The local geology is both dramatic and fascinating. Rocks in this part of North Devon are mainly shales, mudstones and sandstones from the Devonian Period (395-345 million years ago). The Foreland is particularly impressive. A huge red hog-backed cliff, it stands over 200m (600ft) above the sea with massive scree slopes and dominates the view east of Lynmouth (see photograph opposite). To explore it on foot, drive 3km east of Lynmouth on the A39 to Barna Barrow car park. Please stay on the main paths and heed warning notices.

West of Lynton is the extraordinary Valley of Rocks. Spectacular tors and other frost-riven features mark its sides. Arguably, it is the only example of full glacial action in Devon, which lay south of the great ice sheets that covered most of Britain during the last Ice Age.

Erosion by the sea further dismembered the cliffs on the north side of the valley, which is now dry though it was once the bed of the East Lyn. That river left considerable deposits of water-borne rock. To see the Valley of Rocks, you can either drive (see page 30) or walk (see page 18).

The East and West Lyn meet at Lynmouth. Powerful and fast flowing even in the summer, they are most spectacular in spate – and dangerous too, as the 1952 flood disaster proved (see page 10).

During the last Ice Age, when huge volumes of melt water rushed down from Exmoor every spring, conditions on the East and West Lyn were similar to rivers in the Rocky Mountains of North America today. The erosive power of these rivers was and still is greatly increased by the boulders and scree they carry. Indeed, rocks are still strewn all along their banks. Gaining speed and force in their steep descent from Exmoor, the East and West Lyn have carved deep gorges in their lower reaches.

Whilst both gorges can be seen from the roads into Lynton and Lynmouth, the best views are from Watersmeet, a 2 km drive or walk from Lynmouth. Take the footpath down to the National Trust tea rooms to see the river and some of its waterfalls – or follow the beautiful bankside path from Lynmouth (see page 16). The best waterfall of all is Glen Lyn in Lynmouth (entrance fee).

Tourism on Exmoor

A strange double twist of fate created the tourist industry that is the mainstay of the economy of the twin villages today. The first involved a fish and the second a war.

The humble herring had flourished in the Bristol Channel for as long as people could remember. Vast shoals had been caught, dried, salted, and smoked. They were exported to all parts of the country and the continent, providing a good living for those involved in the industry. For some unexplained reason in the late 1700s the fish stocks declined and almost disappeared completely. Times became very hard for the villages and poverty was widespread.

At the time a popular pastime for the very rich was to visit the cities and historical sites of Europe. For young men in particular, the 'Grand Tour' was seen as completing their education. By the 1790s, dramatic scenery was also in vogue, in particular the Alps. When war with France broke out in 1793, continental travel was curtailed. Wealthy travellers were forced to seek alternative places at home to visit. The Lake District, Snowdonia and other regions that have now become National Parks were favoured.

Exmoor, being very picturesque, became popular with artists and writers looking for inspiration. A lifeline had been thrown and the people of Lynmouth and Lynton grabbed at it with both hands.

Two prints, from about 1830, showing Lynmouth's 'Alpine' scenery

Accommodation was very scarce. There was just one small public house, The Crown, in Lynton. A local man, William Litson, realised that there was money to be made and quite quickly built two additional inns, The Globe and The Valley of Rocks Hotel. These were soon to be followed by other hotels and boarding houses.

Although the problem of where to stay had been resolved, reaching Lynmouth was a major obstacle. The two main methods were by horse-drawn coach or by boat. Such roads as existed were little more than rutted dusty tracks in summer and muddy lanes in winter. Because of the steep hills frequent stops had to be made to change the coach horses whose lives were sadly very short.

The sea journey was a popular alternative. To travel here by steamer from Bristol was quicker and cheaper than the overland route. But again it was not without its problems. The sea can be very rough in the Bristol Channel and as Lynmouth did not have a pier passengers had to be brought to shore by a small rowing boat. There were times when the sea was too rough for this to be possible. A plan in 1885 to build a pier at Lynmouth led to speculative building in the area but the project came to nothing.

A rail link was established in 1895 from Barnstaple but it was a narrow gauge line making for a slow journey. The line closed in 1935, by which time the motor coach and private car were a quicker alternative. Wider car ownership made the villages ever more accessible.

The Overland Launch

Late in the afternoon of 12 January 1899 a violent storm was raging in the Bristol Channel. The barque *Forrest Hall* with a crew of eighteen was under tow from Bristol to Liverpool. When she was just west of Ilfracombe the tow line parted and she was left floundering and was being blown back up the Channel by the increasing violence of the storm.

At 7pm a telegraph message was received at Lynmouth Post Office saying that a vessel was showing distress signals off Gore Point, Porlock, and as the Watchet lifeboat was unable to attend would the Lynmouth lifeboat attempt a rescue. It was quite apparent that conditions were too bad even to attempt a launch from Lynmouth. To the utter amazement of the crowd that had gathered, coxswain Jack Crocome announced that they would launch from Porlock.

This meant hauling the 3 1/2 ton boat the 22 km (14 miles) overland to Porlock. Within the hour, 20 horses and many strong men were assembled and the *Louisa* on her wheeled carriage was pulled out of the village. Almost immediately they encountered the first of the many obstacles they were to face, Countisbury Hill, nearly 3 km (1 3/4 miles) in length and rising to 300 m (1000 ft). When they reached the summit a number of the men, realising the enormity of the task, gave up and turned for home.

Twenty of the more determined continued and were to face a series of formidable problems. Sections of the road were too narrow for the carriage to pass, so walls were demolished. In places where the road was impassable the boat was taken from the carriage and hauled across the fields.

Some eight hours later the almost exhausted procession reached the top of Porlock Hill. Nothing as heavy as the *Louisa* had ever gone down this notorious 1 in 4 (25%) hill. Drag anchors and brake horses were employed and the men fought to stop the load from careering down the hill. At the bottom, it was necessary to remove a section of house roof to enable the carriage to make the final turn.

Journey's end finally came at 6.30 am, when they reached Porlock Weir, but their night was not yet over. They immediately launched into the big waves and after a search finally sighted the *Forrest Hall*. As she was no longer in immediate danger they stood by until her original tug arrived to take her back in tow. Because of the rough seas

A re-enactment of the Overland Launch to mark its centenary

it was decided to take her across the Bristol Channel to the Welsh port of Barry, until the storm had abated. The *Louisa* was also taken in tow in case the line severed again.

The following morning the lifeboat was towed back across the Channel to her home port of Lynmouth. She was met by cheering crowds who had gathered on the quayside.

The 'Overland Launch' has gone down in the annals of the Lifeboat Institution as one of the greatest feats of endurance in their long history.

The 1952 Flood

The item which dominated BBC radio news broadcasts on 16 August 1952 was that a terrible flood had claimed many lives in a small North Devon harbour village most people had never heard of. The Lynmouth tragedy was at the time the largest loss of life by floods in Britain's history.

Those people who did know of Lynmouth had probably holidayed or honeymooned there, and were wondering how such a dreadful event could have occurred in a peaceful Exmoor village with a small river meandering quietly through its centre. Gradually over the following week the enormity of the disaster became apparent, with most people seeing it on the cinema newsreels. (Few people owned televisions, and outside broadcasts were still in their infancy.)

The first two weeks of August 1952 were very wet. Holidaymakers looking for the sunshine in Devon had been disappointed. Days of rain had left Exmoor waterlogged, with the rivers and their feeder streams at high levels. The 15th of August dawned with the promise of a little sunshine, but by mid morning it had started to rain steadily. By noon the skies were dark enough for lights to be switched on in the houses and the heavy rain was incessant. Those who were out in the village could see that the river levels were quickly rising; the visitors found it worth watching but the locals, who had seen the river level rise before and then drop again equally fast, got on with their business.

At about 5pm a tremendous cloudburst started and continued for over an hour. Few local people had ever witnessed such a downpour and even they began to take notice. By 7pm, when a report of flooding on the Lynton to Simonsbath Road was received at Lynton Police Station, things were beginning to look serious. From then on many calls were received indicating that the situation was getting worse.

Lynton's electricity was generated by water power fed via a small canal to the generating station. At 7.30pm the canal was damaged and generation was switched over to the diesel back-up. At 9pm this also failed, when the generating hall was flooded.

As the water level rose in the village and started to enter the houses and hotels, some people tried to save their possessions but most just fled and made for higher ground. At the Lyndale Hotel, staff and guests hurried upstairs, eventually only finding refuge on the third

An aerial view of the devastation

floor from the rising water. They spent the night in a state of terror, with the building being shaken by gigantic boulders smashed into it by the flood water. They were expecting the whole structure to be swept away at any moment and themselves with it.

At dawn the full horror was revealed. Lynmouth looked like a First World War battlefield and as if buildings had been blown open by shell fire. What was left of the streets was strewn with massive boulders, trees, wrecked cars and debris from the buildings.

Thirty-four people lost their lives that night in and around Lynmouth. Ninety-three buildings were destroyed or had to be demolished, 28 bridges were destroyed and 132 cars were wrecked or swept away into the sea. It would be two years before the village was reconstructed to how you see it today, substantially redesigned to

The Cliff Railway

Although Lynton and Lynmouth are only 140 m (450 feet) apart, it is an almost vertical cliff face that separates them. A modern car should have no problems in climbing the 25% road gradient in the valley, but before the age of the car the cliff presented great problems for the inhabitants of the twin villages, particularly as most of the trade goods arrived in Lynmouth by boat and had to be taken up to Lynton.

Packhorses and donkeys were used to convey life's necessities between the villages. Tourists also were carried between the villages on the backs of these poor creatures. It soon became apparent that the problem would need to be addressed if tourism was to flourish.

A plan was outlined to build a waterpower lift between the villages and finance was sought to build it. Sir Thomas Hewitt who lived in Lynton was a friend of the entrepreneur and publisher Sir George Newnes. The scheme was put to Sir George and he agreed to provide most of the capital required.

The accomplished engineer George Croydon Marks (later Baron Marks of Woolwich) who had designed and constructed Britain's first cliff railway, which opened in 1884 at Saltburn-by-the-Sea, was engaged in the project. A local builder Bob Jones was employed for the construction.

The work took over a year to complete and involved the removal of hundreds of tons of rock from the proposed route. A final gradient of 1 in 1.76 was agreed and 860 feet (263 m) of railway line was laid. The two cars are joined by cables going round large wheels at the top and bottom stations. The system works on the counter-balance principle, using water as the weight. The water is taken via pipes from the West Lyn River and stored in a large reservoir near the top station. Water is held in the tanks beneath each car and on a given bell signal water is discharged from the lower car until it is lighter than the top car. When the brakes are taken off, the top car slowly descends, pulling the bottom one up. This process is then repeated for each journey. The railway was opened on Easter Monday 1890 to much celebration and brass band playing.

Needless to say there are a number of independent braking systems to ensure passenger safety. In its long history it has always had a one hundred percent safety record and no visit to Lynton and Lynmouth is complete without a ride on its famous cliff railway.

The Town Hall

One October day in 1897 the Town Council meeting was interrupted by a local builder bearing a telegram announcing that Sir George Newnes proposed to give the community a magnificent Town Hall. It took two years to build, using local oak and stone, and cost the then enormous sum of £20,000.

If you look at the building you will have difficulty in deciding in which architectural style it is built – 'municipal architecture in a holiday spirit' according to Pevsner's *Buildings of Devon*. In truth it is a clever combination of 'English manorial', Gothic and Tudor, reflecting the concept of *Tit-Bits*, Sir George's famous magazine. It is usually open and a visit is recommended. The main hall on the first floor, reached up the very grand staircase, has an impressive oak-trussed roof. The building is well used by local people and is licensed for marriages.

The Lyn and Exmoor Museum

St Vincent Cottage in Market Street is thought to be the oldest domestic building in Lynton. It now houses a charming collection of curiosities, kitchen appliances, agricultural tools, local historical items, a man trap and a ghost! The museum was founded in 1962 focusing on local history and nearly all the exhibits have been donated by local residents.

Sinai Hill in Lynton – one of the steepest hills to drive in England. Going from 1 in 4 (25%) at the bottom to 1 in 3 (33%) at the top, it is not for the faint-hearted!

The Valley of Rocks Hotel

The Valley of Rocks Hotel that you see today is on the site of the original Valley of Rocks Inn built in 1807 by William Litson to meet the growing need for accommodation. When it was constructed there were virtually no other buildings west of it towards the Valley of Rocks. Almost all the buildings you see today are the result of Victorian and Edwardian expansion of the village.

In 1887 the hotel was owned by John Crook, who built an extension. The final stage of its development was completed in 1889 by the then owners, the Lynton & Lynmouth Property Company. They demolished the old part of the hotel, built a new wing and added a superb hall and an imposing entrance. The hotel became the fashionable place for the 'gentry' to stay in Lynton. It is now owned by The Shearings Holiday Group.

A walk from Lynmouth to Watersmeet and back

Distance: 6km (3¹/₂ miles)
Or 11km (6³/₄ miles) to the Rockford Inn

The walk to this famous beauty spot starts at Lynmouth and passes along one of Britain's deepest river-cut gorges. Its sides are lined with sessile oak and a few rare whitebeams. Among the birds you might spot are dippers, wagtails and herons. In late Autumn, large salmon can be seen on their way upriver to spawn.

Start from the Lyndale car park, next to the road bridge in Lynmouth. Continue upriver, passing the footbridge on your left and the site of the hydro-electric power station (destroyed by the flood) on your right. Also on your right you will see Middleham Memorial Gardens, where a row of cottages was washed away.

Continue walking upstream, crossing the river as directed, until you reach Watersmeet. The East Lyn river and Hoar Oak Water meet here, and there are waterfalls just above the junction. Watersmeet House was built in 1832 as a fishing and hunting lodge. It is now owned by the National Trust and is a tearoom and gift shop.

For the return, start on the Watersmeet House side of the river, and follow the signs back to Lynmouth.

The walk can be extended by continuing along the beautiful river-bank path for a further 2.5 km (1 1/2) miles, to the Rockford Inn (see photograph above), a pleasantly unpretentious pub which brews its own beer. To do this, turn left as you leave the National Trust tearoom and head upriver, signed FISHERMAN'S PATH ROCKFORD & BRENDON. Just after Rockford Lodge, cross a footbridge to the pub.

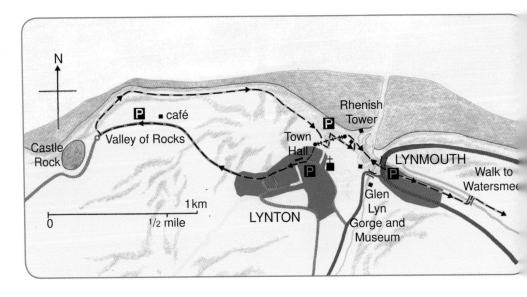

A walk exploring the villages

Distance: 4km (2 1/2 miles)

Start from Lyndale car park – the car park near to the A39 road bridge. At this point the East and West Lyn Rivers meet. Make your way over to where the West Lyn meets the East and you will find The Glen Lyn Gorge Power of Water Exhibition (next to Shelley's Hotel). Electricity has been generated by water power in Lynmouth since 1890 and it was one of the first places in the country to have electric street lighting.

The generating plant was approximately 200m (220 yards) upstream on the right hand side of the East Lyn River. It was washed away in the 1952 flood. At Glen Lyn Gorge there is a new hydro-electric power-generating plant feeding electricity into the National Grid. In the exhibition there are a number of water-powered machines including a water canon, great fun for adults and children alike.

Make your way back to the bridge, turn left into Riverside Road and walk down towards the harbour. Just past the Bath Hotel you will find a building which houses an exhibition to the flood disaster. It is rather fitting that it should be there, since it is the site of the old lifeboat house, which was lost to the flood waters. A little further on is the Rising Sun Hotel. This thatched 14th century building is an historic smugglers' inn. It has been transformed over the years into an elegant harbourside hostelry. Its oak panelled dining room offers magnificent views of the harbour.

The West Lyn River, now used to generate electricity. There are two markers on trees upstream which indicate the almost unbelievable level the water reached in the 1952 flood

Below: the Rising Sun Hotel in Lynmouth

The harbour at Lynmouth, with the Rhenish Tower on the right

Opposite the Rising Sun Hotel is the Rhenish Tower. The original tower, fancifully based on the design of castles on the River Rhine in Germany, was built to house a tank which fed sea water to an establishment near The Bath Hotel. This provided sea water baths, considered beneficial to health by the Victorians. What you see today is a faithful reproduction of the original structure which was destroyed in the flood.

Now make your way up to Lynton. Although there is a footpath near to the Rising Sun, it is very steep so I strongly recommend that you go up by the Cliff Railway. You will find the bottom station a short distance west of the Rhenish Tower. Don't purchase a return ticket as you will be walking down on your return. From the upper station, you will find that the railway approach road brings you out onto Lee Road. Turn left and walk past The Valley of Rocks Hotel to St Mary's Church, which is usually unlocked.

The view from the Church Yard is breathtaking. Below you are Lynmouth Harbour and Manor Green, ahead and just to the right are Foreland Point and Countisbury. Fully to your right is Watersmeet Valley. On most days the coast of South Wales can easily be seen and

Porthcawl, just east of due north at a distance of 27 km (17 miles), is often visible. On very clear days Swansea and the Mumbles, 44 km (27 miles) away and just west of due north can also be seen.

Leaving the churchyard turn right past The Valley of Rocks Hotel and the Town Hall. Approximately 400 m further on the right is the Convent of the Poor Clares. Five sisters of this order arrived here from France in 1904. Following temporary accommodation in Lynmouth the convent was built and opened in 1910. The Italianate church is usually open and is beautiful.

Continue walking west and in about ten minutes you will be at the head of the Valley of Rocks. (See page 4 for a very brief explanation of its geology.) This valley has been described as one of the seven wonders of the West Country and it is a fascinating place. Many of the rock formations on the north side are named, Ragged Jack, Chimney Rock and The Devils Cheese Ring to mention but three.

Have you ever seen a more spectacular setting for a cricket ground? In 1891 Sir George Newnes paid for the levelling in the valley to provide a cricket ground for the villages and the game has been played in these dramatic surroundings ever since.

Some inhabitants of the valley you are almost sure to see are the goats. Wild goats have lived here on and off for at least 400 years and

probably a lot longer than that. RD Blackmore in his novel *Lorna Doone* writes of an encounter with one of them by Jan Ridd. Towards the end of the 19th century they appeared to have died out and the valley was restocked from Sir Thomas Hewitt's Lynton estate, but the current herd is descended from three feral goats from the Cheviots released in December 1976, after cold winters in the 1960s had killed off their predecessors.

The goats are not universally popular, since they have learned to tiptoe across the cattle grid and then damage gardens in Lynton. Views on all sides of the issue can become decidedly heated.

Exmoor ponies also occasionally visit the valley, and a small herd can sometimes be found grazing freely.

At the far end of the valley is a roundabout and to its right is a footpath. Take this path signposted LYNTON. You are now on a section of the South West Coast Path. The entire path is 1014 km long (630 miles) and goes from Minehead all the way around the South-West peninsula to Poole. Your walk will give you some wonderful views across the Bristol Channel and for a short time you should be able to see Foreland Lighthouse on the end of Countisbury Point.

After about 1000 m (2/3 mile) you will go through a gate onto North Walk. Passing three hotels on your right you will cross a bridge over

the Cliff Railway, with the view shown above. Just past this bridge there is a turning on your left that will take you down to Lynmouth, where this walk ends.

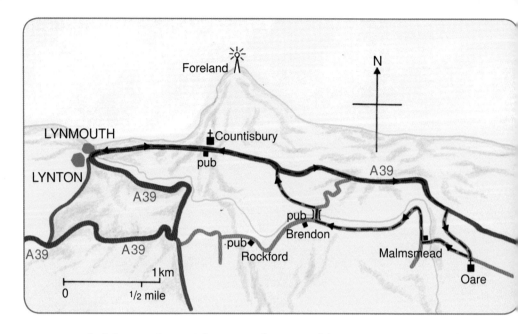

A drive to Countisbury, Malmsmead (Lorna Doone Farm), Oare and Brendon

Distance: 18km (11 miles)

This route is not suitable for large motor caravans.

Start from Lyndale Bridge at the centre of Lynmouth. Cross the East Lyn river bridge onto the A39, signed MINEHEAD. You now begin the long ascent of Countisbury Hill (25% in parts) which provides wonderful views on the left for the passenger but the driver would be well advised to keep a sharp lookout for the sheep that like to lie in the road. The sandy beach below you is Sillery Sands, reached via a winding footpath or at a very low tide from Lynmouth.

After 2.4km (1½ miles) you will reach the hamlet of Countisbury. It is dominated by the Blue Ball Inn, one of the oldest on Exmoor, which in recent years was called the Exmoor Sandpiper but has now reverted to its older name. It was used as a staging post to change the coach horses after their long haul up from Lynmouth.

You are now almost 300m (1000ft) above the sea and to your left are Countisbury Church and Foreland Point, beneath which is the lighthouse, today unmanned and automated. The old lighthouse keepers' cottages are owned by the National Trust and rented as holiday cottages.

By parking at the Barna Barrow car park, 400m (¼ mile) beyond

the Blue Ball, you can take a short walk with superb views (see the photograph above) out to the coast path and along to the right, but it is not possible to reach the lighthouse from the coast path, and in any case it is not open to the public.

RD Blackmore published *Lorna Doone* in 1869. After a stuttering start it eventually became a 'classic'. Sometimes it is hard to believe that it is a work of fiction as Blackmore cleverly weaves factual locations and characters into the plot. He also compresses local folklore and known historical events spanning two hundred years into the short time period of the novel. It remains a classic love story, of a young Exmoor farmer determined to right the wrongs in his land and win the heart of Lorna. Blackmore wrote many books but *Lorna Doone* is the only one still in print. It has been made into a number of films and adapted for television.

Countisbury Church, stoutly built to withstand the winter gales, is one of the highest on Exmoor and probably the only one not to have electricity. It is normally unlocked if you wish to visit.

Leaving Countisbury, continue on A39 for nearly 6 km (3 1/2 miles). The beautiful Brendon Valley is on your right. The area of Exmoor beyond the valley is known as Brendon Common, with The Chains – a high ridge covered with blanket bog – in the far distance.

Take the turning on the right signed OARE. After 1.5 km (nearly a mile) descending this steep hill you will reach Oare, with the church right in front of you. This was the location where in the novel *Lorna Doone* the heroine was shot (not fatally) on her wedding day.

Obviously a visit to Oare Church is a must. When you are ready to leave, take the road signed MALMSMEAD, which you will reach after 1.25 km (3/4 mile). The bridge, ford and Lorna Doone Farm shop and tearoom must be one of the most photographed locations on Exmoor. Cross the narrow bridge or drive through the ford, turn right and you will find a car park on the right hand side.

Leaving Malmsmead take the road signed BRENDON. After a drive of 3 km (2 miles) passing through beautiful Southern Wood you will reach Brendon. This pretty little village sits alongside the East Lyn River. There is a tea room near the cross roads, and a pub called The Stag Hunters a few hundred metres beyond. Take the turning on the right signed COUNTISBURY LYNMOUTH, cross the stone bridge and after approximately 1.4 km (1500 yards) you will reach the A39. Turn left and drive the 4 km (2 1/2 miles) back to Lynmouth.

The bridge and ford at Malmsmead, beside Lorna Doone Farm

The Lynton & Barnstaple Railway

With the growth of tourism there was a clamour in the twin villages to have a rail link to the main line. Several proposed routes were considered and finally a line to Barnstaple was chosen. As the route needed to negotiate many tight bends, a narrow gauge line (1ft 11½in) was the preferred option. This proved to be a bad choice and eventually contributed to the closure of the line. Once again it was Sir George Newnes who was the principal financial backer.

The line was to be nearly 31km (19 miles) long from a station on the outskirts of Lynton to Barnstaple Town Station. Five new stations were planned, Lynton, Woody Bay, Blackmoor, Bratton Fleming and Chelfham (pronounced 'Chellam'), as well as halts at Caffyns, Parracombe, and Snapper.

Construction by James Nuttall of Manchester began in September 1895. The work was much harder than expected, with considerable amounts of blasting being required. Costs began to spiral and the final figure was almost double the original estimate. The grand opening was held in Lynton on 11 May 1898 with much celebration.

From the beginning, there were many problems with the railway. Firstly it was very slow. With seven stops between Barnstaple and Lynton, the journey time was up to 1½ hours. Secondly Sir George

Newnes understandably did not want a viaduct across the valley at Lynton, which would have linked the new line to the Cliff Railway, so the station was situated on the outskirts of the village, at a considerable distance from Lynmouth where most visitors wished to go. The railway never did make money and was closed in 1935, unable to compete with the private car and motor coach.

The story of this picturesque little railway does not end there. In 1979 a trust was set up (later replaced by a company) to restore the railway, with the ultimate aim of linking Lynton to Barnstaple by train once again. In 2004, a short section of the line was reopened, and later extended, based on Woody Bay Station.

The station itself has been restored to a very high standard. There is a small museum and steam train trips can be taken on the section of line that has been re-laid. Refreshments are available as are railway books and toys.

Lynton Station is now a private house but is outwardly little changed from its days as a station.

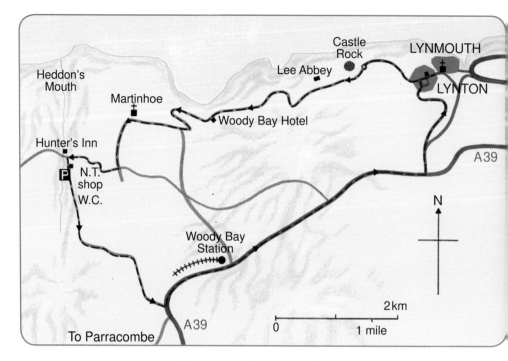

A drive to Lee Abbey, Woody Bay and Hunters Inn

Distance: 13 km (8 miles)

Please note, this drive involves very narrow lanes, with rather too few passing places and seriously steep hills. Beyond the roundabout in the Valley of the Rocks, it is unsuitable for caravans or motor homes.

Start from St Mary's Church in Lynton and drive west (slightly uphill) along Lee Road, passing the Town Hall on your right. Continue ahead, keeping right. After approximately 1.5 km (1 mile) you will drive over a cattle grid into the Valley of the Rocks (see pages 4 and 21).

There is a picnic area car park on the left, and another car park on the right just beyond the cricket ground. Continue past the roundabout. When you cross another cattle grid, you will be entering the grounds of Lee Abbey, which is on your right. It was built around 1840 as a private house, and never has been an abbey, though the land is said to have once belonged to Cistercian monks. By coincidence it is now owned by the Church of England and is used as a Christian holiday and conference centre. At the far end of Lee Abbey grounds there is a car park and a footpath to Lee Bay (photograph opposite) where there is a beautiful cove with a sandy beach at low tide. Dogs are not allowed between April and October.

To continue driving along this road you will need to pay a small toll in the 'honesty box'. After paying, carry on towards Woody Bay on a very narrow winding road, with passing points. About 400 m (¹/₄ mile) after passing the Woody Bay Hotel, there is a car park. A track opposite, long, steep and unsuitable for motor vehicles, takes you down to secluded Woody Bay with its superb shingle beach.

Continue up the road from the car park and follow the sign to MARTINHOE, with an interesting church. You will see a gravestone on

---

In 1885, Colonel Benjamin Lake, a London solicitor and property developer, bought the Manor at Woody Bay. He had a grand design to develop Woody Bay into a second Lynmouth. He bought up property, did some building work, and planned a cliff railway similar to Lynmouth's and a pier to attract the steamer traffic of the Bristol Channel. The pier was completed in 1897 but was badly damaged in a violent storm three years later.

With mounting debts his grand schemes started to fail, and in 1901 he was charged at the Old Bailey with misappropriating clients' money entrusted to him as a solicitor, and sentenced to twelve years in prison. His Woody Bay estate had to be sold off to pay his debts and he died a broken man in 1909.

Woody Bay never did become another Lynmouth, but has remained a beautifully peaceful place in its own right.

Martinhoe Church

Heddon's Mouth, once used as a landing point to bring limestone from south Wales. Limestone was added to local soils to counteract their acidity. There is a rebuilt lime kiln close to the sea shore

the left side of the churchyard to 'Lorna Doone'. Continue along this road and take the first turning on the right, signed HUNTERS INN. This is quite a winding road and one of the steepest in the area. At the foot of the hill, I suggest you park in the National Trust car park to the left. There is a gift shop which serves ice-cream. The Hunters Inn Hotel was originally a thatched building, which suffered a devastating fire in 1895. It was rebuilt, and enlarged, in 1900.

To the right of the hotel is a footpath which follows the river to Heddon's Mouth.

Leaving the car park, take the road for PARRACOMBE. After about 3 km (2 miles) which feels like rather further, you will reach a T-junction. Turn left, A39. Opposite the petrol station at Barbrook, turn left and follow signs back to Lynton.